Coloring book

For

Kids

coloring and teaching numbers

This coloring book belongs to:

0
Zero

One

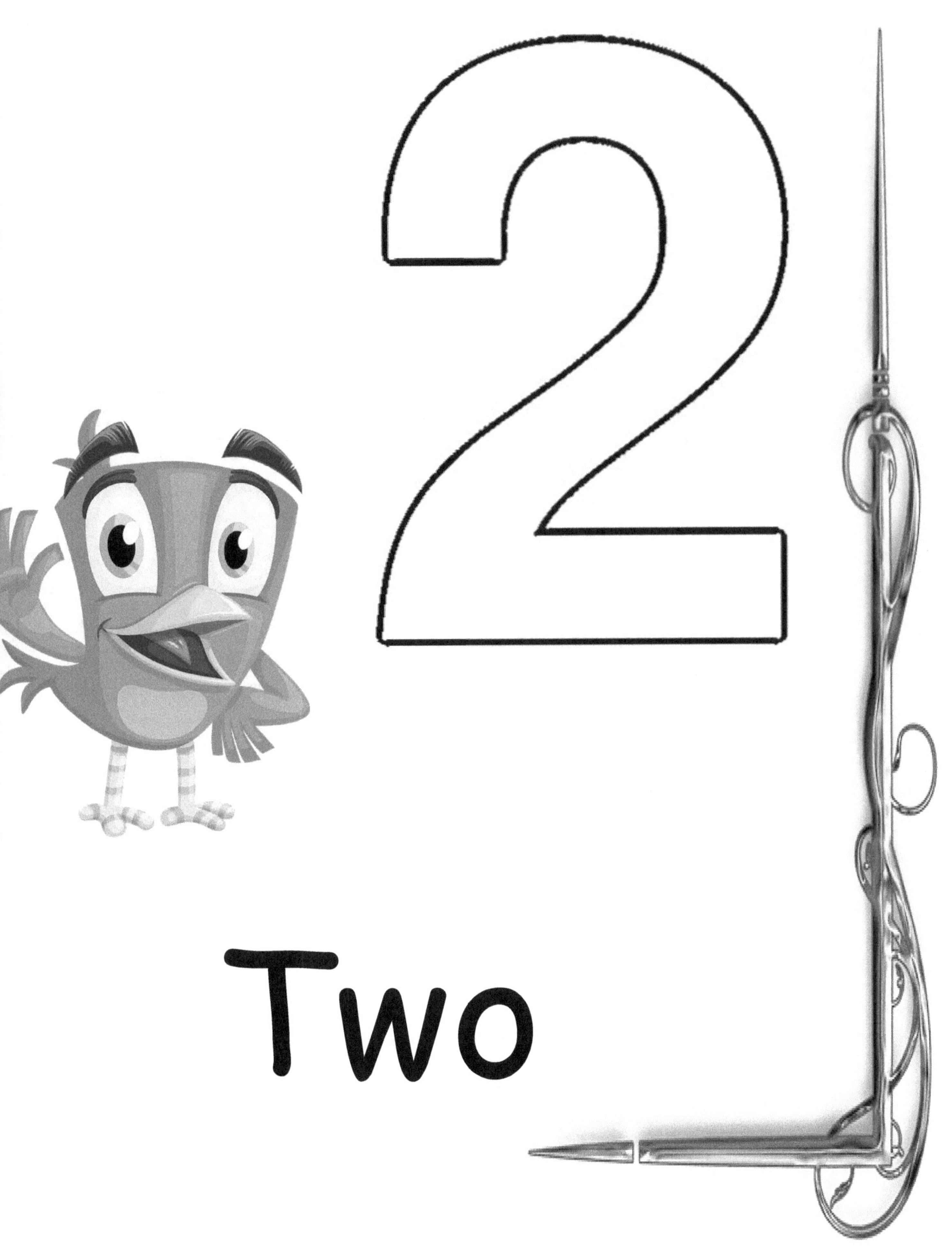

2

Two

3

Three

4
Four

5

Five

6
Six

7
Seven

8
Eight

9

Nine

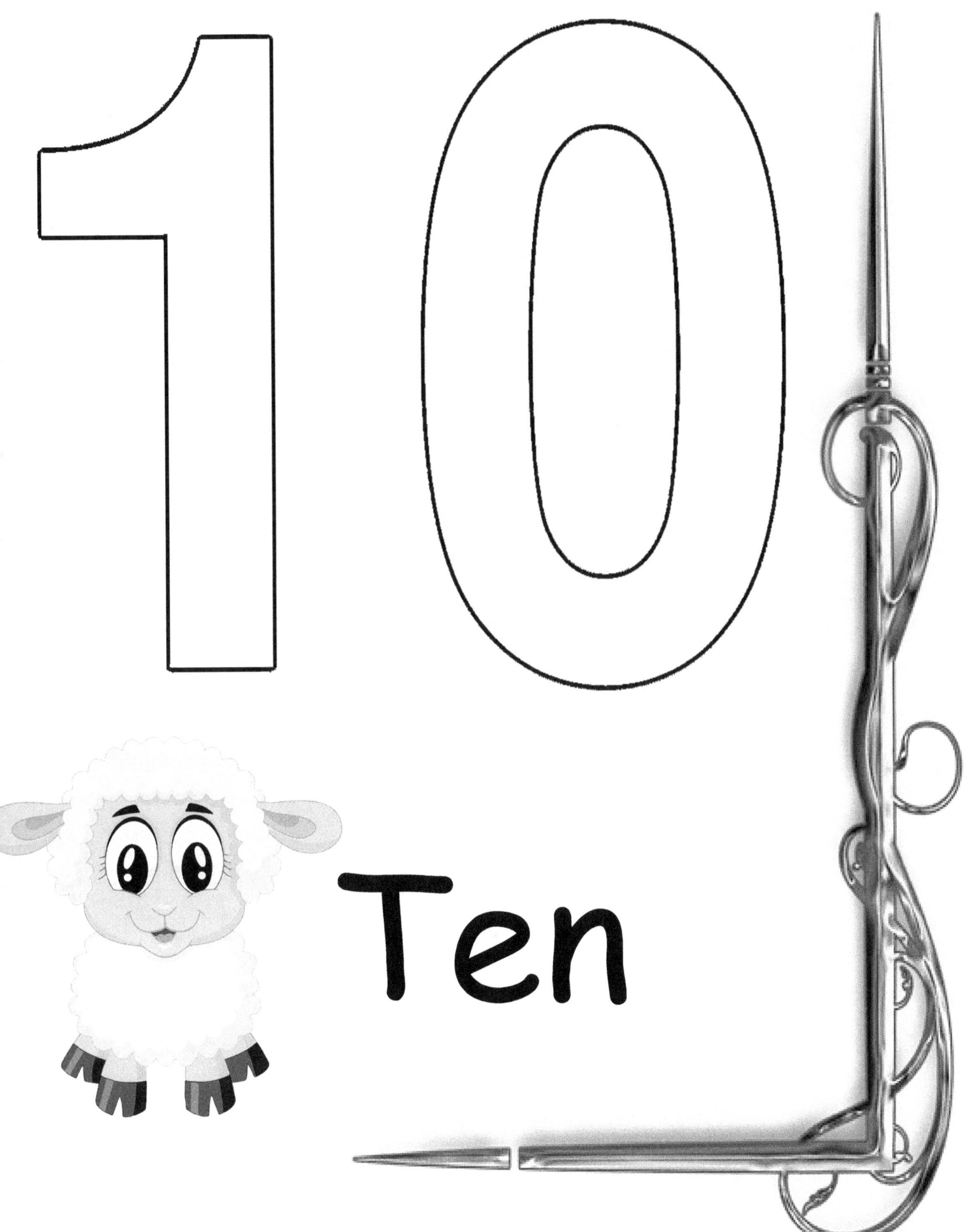

10

Ten

11
Eleven

Twelve

13

Thirteen

14

Fourteen

Fifteen

16
Sixteen

17

Seventeen

18

Eighteen

19

Nineteen

20
Twenty

21
Twenty
one

22

Twenty two

23

Twenty
three

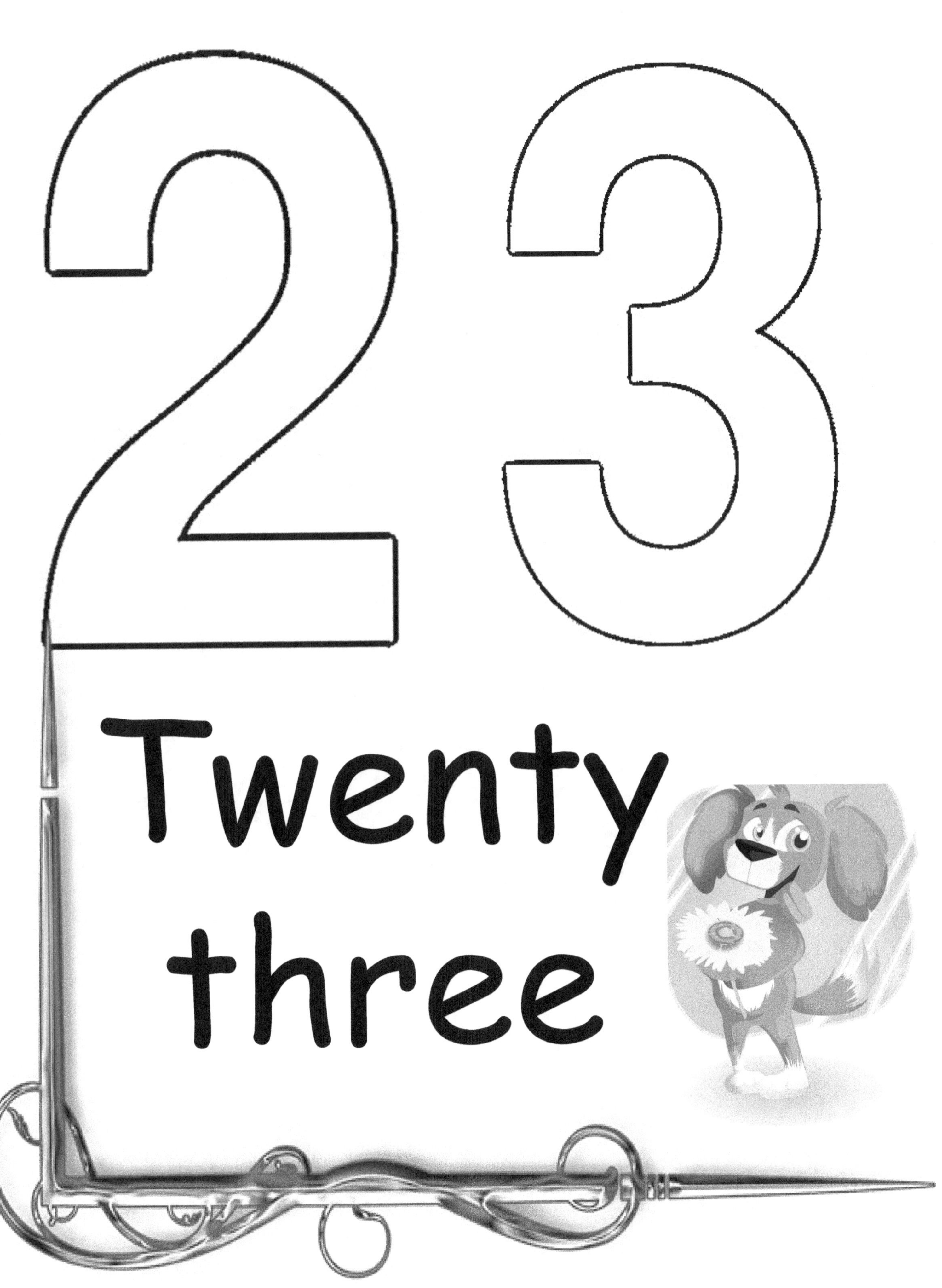

2 4
Twenty
four

25
Twenty
five

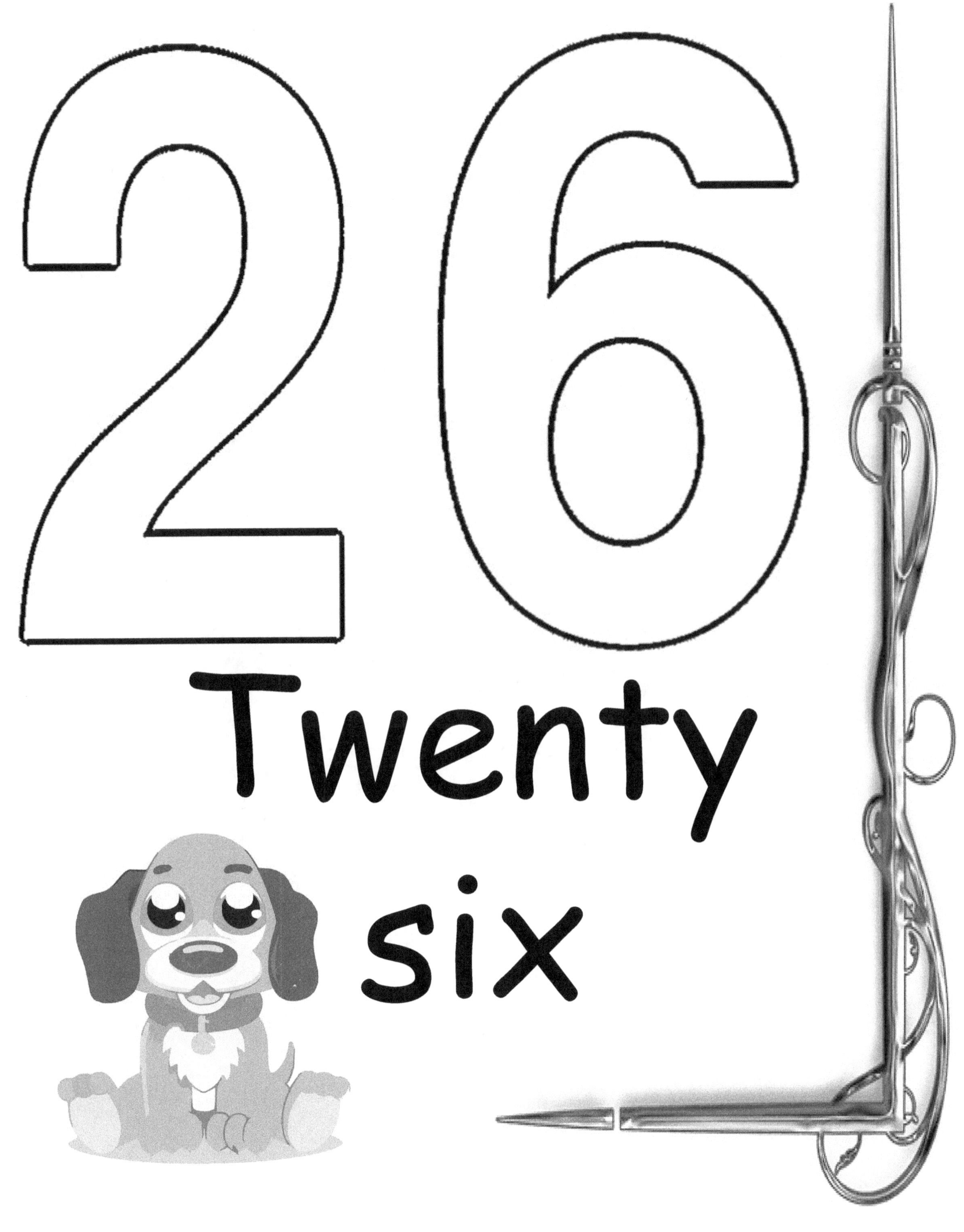

26
Twenty
six

27
Twenty
seven

28
Twenty
eight

29

Twenty
nine

30
Thirty

Well, it looks like you have finished coloring the numbers. You are a hero!!

Now write the numbers you learned here:

Good you are making progress

Right now ! Try writing the numbers in letters on the next page

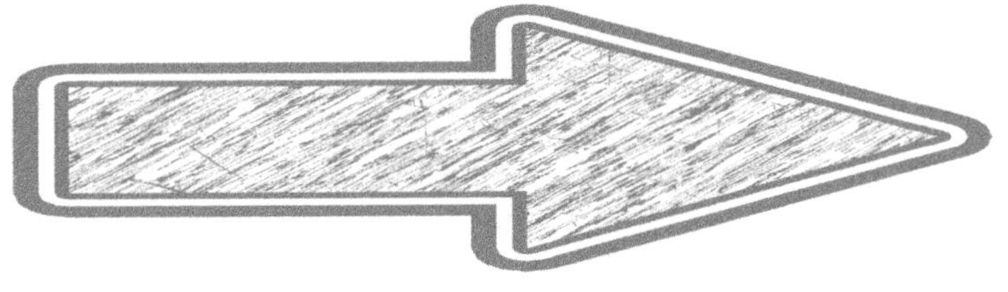

Good bye, hero

I will miss you a lot